MAHJONG MADE EASY: A Step-by-Step Beginner's Guide to Playing and Winning

Meghan Corey

Table of Contents

CHAPTER ONE

INTRODUCTION

Mah Jong is an old Chinese game. As time elapsed on, in better places different kinds of the game bounced up like Cantonese, Japanese, western regular, Taiwanese, Filipino, Fijian and Vietnamese. Accordingly, one should be know about the way that it has different assortments. Overall standard principles were made to control the developments and in 2002, First World Mah Jong Title was held. The best strategy for getting capacity with the game is by basically playing it. Comparatively with any extra games, the more you work on something, the more prominent power you gain in it. Here besides a tantamount rule applies. Least of two players should begin the game. The hardware of the game merges various types of tiles-circle suit, bamboo suit, character suit, wind tiles, winged snake tiles, blossom tiles and joker tiles. There are all around 144 tiles endlessly out in any case 136, 144, 148 or 152 are in addition permitted.

A full game has 16 hands of play in 4 rounds named after 4 headings and every player has a specific bearing. Each of the players tosses the dice and the player with the most raised score will rush to begin the game. Resulting stage is to make the wall, and that means to organize the tiles in a stack. The tiles are blended and facilitated in 18 stacks in a level line before every player as a square. The stack is then broken and every player gets 13 tiles. Various tiles are known as the wall and kept in the center. Every player begins to dispose of the tiles and draws from the wall. Objective is to make 4 sets and a couple; get-together of 3 industrious same suit tiles or 3 unclear tiles or a ton of 4 of a sort. Each point has a specific money related worth that is predefined by players. Whoever does this at first is the champ and in the event that the wall gets depleted without a victory, the game is a draw. There are different combinations in rules and scoring other than there are even teaches for testing unequivocal guidelines. Mah Jong is a jumbled and a "card sharks down" and a fan of the game should be taught with it. Mahjong is a striking

Chinese game played with sets of tiles. Comparably as other remarkable games, mahjong has different close by collections, from the Chinese winning breeze design to American mahjong with uncommon bingo-like scoring cards. Examine on to figure out a smart method for playing mahjong utilizing the game's critical principles and strategies, which are equivalent across most different assortments.

CHAPTER TWO

THE BEST PROCEDURE TO PLAY MAHJONG

American Mahjong

Mahjong is played with four players organized around a table however there are assortments with three players. Players mix the tiles, cast the dice, and perform customs including the piece of tiles. Then, the trading of tiles starts. The fundamental individual to match a hand of 14 tiles and call "mahjong" closes the game. Tiles are then scored and not totally settled

Parts

The fundamental game has 136 tiles, including 36 characters, 36 bamboos, and

36 circles, which are the suits. These are, in like manner, separated into four approaches of numbers 1 to 9 in each suit. There are in addition 16 breeze tiles and 12 winged snake tiles. Many sets likewise unite an extra eight tiles with four sprouts and four seasons, yet these are not required in the significant game. One courses of action of dice is utilized to pick the arrangement. Having four racks is discretionary.

Objective

The objective of the game is to get a mahjong, which contains getting all of the 14 of your tiles into four sets and one set. A couple is two unclear tiles. A set can either be a "pung," which is three muddled tiles, or a "chow," which is a run of three sequential numbers in a similar suit. A solitary tile can't be involved there of mind straightaway.

Game-plan

Pick a beginning vendor. In Chinese custom, the four breeze tiles are changed face down and sorted out some way to the players. Players then, sit as per their tile and sit clockwise in the sales north, west, south, east. East beginning stages as the dealer. Present day players may basically throw the dice to pick the seller. All tiles are patched up together, and the players construct a mass of 34 face-down tiles before themselves, 17 tiles in length and two tiles high. The outcome ought to be a huge square mass of tiles in the mark of union of the table. The vendor throws the dice and counts that many tiles from the right edge of their wall, and separates the wall by then to start supervising tiles from the left of that spot and going clockwise. Every player gets 13 tiles, with the vendor beginning with an extra fourteenth tile. Every player then, at that point, facilitates their own tiles so they can see them and different players can't. Racks are consistently utilized in this way. The vendor then, disposes of one tile, and play begins to the side of the dealer.

Play

Before your turn, you should give different players a few minutes to guarantee the most really disposed of tile.

The fundamental goal goes to any player who can guarantee the disposed of tile to finish a mahjong. A player who can do these claims the tile, then, uncovers the triumphant hand of 14 tiles.

Blockading that, any player can guarantee the disposed of tile to finish a pung. The player says "pung", and some time later uncovers the two matching tiles that match the dispose of. For instance, expecting the disposed of tile was the 7 of bamboo, and the player had two more bamboo 7s on the rack, that player would call "pung". While calling pung, a player turns the finished pung (with each of the three bamboo 7s, for this situation) face-up, disposes of an alternate tile, and the go passes to one side.

In the event that no one cases the disposed of tile however it finishes a chow for you, you might guarantee it toward the start of your chance by saying "chow". You then should turn your chow face-up, uncovering the finished run (for example 5, 6, 7 of bamboo) as in the pung model above. You then dispose of an alternate tile and play goes on as expected. In the event that the dispose of doesn't finish a set for you, then on your turn you draw the following tile from the wall (going left). Except if this gives you a mahjong, you then dispose of a tile face-up. Note that main the most as of late disposed of tile can be guaranteed.

Kong

A few players likewise play with a "Kong", which are four of a similar tile (like a drawn out pung). Similar guidelines for guaranteeing a disposed of tile apply, however any player finishing a kong promptly draws an additional tile prior to disposing of.

Hand End

The hand closes when someone pronounces mahjong and uncovers a total 14-tile hand of four sets and a couple. On the off chance that no one has uncovered a mahjong when the wall runs out of tiles, the game is viewed as a draw and the seller redeals.

Scoring

Straightforward scoring grants one highlight whoever accomplished the mahjong and won the hand. A lot more perplexing scoring plans exist, which fluctuate generally by locale. Reward point-scoring grants an extra point for not winning by taking a dispose of, or winning with the last tile in the game, or having a pung of mythical serpents. Remarkable scoring scores every pung at 2 places, which is multiplied on the off chance that the pung was not uncovered, multiplied assuming the pung utilized ones or nines, and multiplied two times more assuming the pung was a kong.

Because of the many scoring varieties, players ought to be mindful so as to settle on scoring rules before a game.

THE SYSTEM OF MAHJONG

On the off chance that you have played solitaire mahjong on the web and, played the genuine game in-house with four individuals, you'll without a doubt have seen that the web-based rendition and the genuine variant share nothing practically speaking. Not exclusively are the games entirely unexpected however because of the way that you are playing against real individuals, it adds one more aspect to the game. This is why mahjong is invigorating. You're dashing against your rivals to make a triumphant hand yet you likewise should consider what your tile disposes of will mean for different players. Will it help them or frustrate them?

Assuming that you are know all about the round of mahjong, you will realize that a triumphant hand is made out of making merges of three tiles which can be a bunch of three called a "pung" or a succession of three called a "chow". You really want 4 merges and a couple of copy tiles to finish the hand of 14 tiles. At the point when you initially get going the game, every player is appropriated 13 tiles. You get the fourteenth tile for the success by self-draw or by gathering it from a player dispose of. In any case, in the event that your hand isn't prepared at this point, you can in any case make chows and pungs as you continued looking for a total hand in a similar way by self-draw or getting tile disposes of. In any case, while you can acknowledge a tile for a pung from any of your rivals, you can acknowledge a tile for a chow from the player to one side. For each situation, since you are tolerating a tile from another player, you should uncover that arrangement of pung or chow tiles face up. In the event that you draw a tile for a pung or a chow without help from anyone else, you can keep your tiles stowed away. As may be obvious, without the karma of self-draw on your side, you will require help from your adversaries in making your hand. You should have the option to mask the hand you are fabricating enough so your adversaries will accidentally help you. Alternately, you should have the option to think about the thing your rivals are holding also and keep the tiles you realize they need in your own hand anyway it could diminish your possibilities winning.

The secret to playing mahjong is to realize that when will generally be forceful and take potentially dangerous courses of action to win and when to play guarded but still have the option to figure out wins too. The round of mahjong is really a round of brains against your rivals and for that reason it is such a ton better when you play it with others than alone.

CHAPTER THREE

THE ADVANTAGES OF MAHJONG GAMES

Mahjong games owe their starting point to China and they are played through utilization of tiles. It was only after in the 1920's that its prevalence in nations, for example, the US started. It is a knowledge game and requires a high feeling of focus. While it is a troublesome game to dominate and learn, when a player gets the thought behind it, it turns out to be not difficult to succeed in a boundless way. Normally, these require four players and keeping in mind that this is the situation, there are varieties. There are a few advantages related with it and a portion of these are as featured underneath.

Treatment of Dementia

Mahjong games can be classed as mental games and analysts guarantee that it has the capacity of treating dementia. It requires a high feeling of fixation, arranging, estimation abilities and memory and thusly, a player's memory is constantly honed. Those individuals who play these games have the capacity of creating mental measures and these impacts keep going for a long term if under any circumstance, they skip playing for a month.

Improvement of Mental Capacities

An enormous number of seniors experience the ill effects of dementia at one point in their life and by enjoying this they have a superior possibility guaranteeing that this doesn't occur. This is on the grounds that it levels up memory abilities and helps in keeping the psyche sharp. Generally, they work in a similar way as crossword puzzles. It likewise works on the player's capacity to respond to various sorts of circumstances and this builds the ability of going with quick choices. At the point when this is utilized in the correct way, it likewise means worked on living abilities among people experiencing dementia.

Social Outlet

This is viewed as an optimal social source for individuals from all gatherings and particularly seniors. Socialization is significant for this gathering and due to the advantages referenced before this allows them the opportunity to partake in this end. Whether they decide to play from a senior's home or a nursing place, it fills a similar need and this is viewed as a significant lift.

Multi-age

Individuals from various age gatherings can partake in the advantages related with this game. Youngsters for example, can figure out how to play on the web. Because of the degree of focus it requests, it is viewed as an optimal instructive choice for youngsters. Furthermore, it is viewed as an optimal approach to having a great time while simultaneously creating mental abilities for this age bunch. To appreciate Mahjong games, one must be working out, vital and fortunate also.

YOU NEEDN'T BOTHER WITH TO BE CHINESE TO PLAY MAHJONG GAMES

How might you want to scramble Mahjong tiles without really being on the table to play them? The game has adopted an entirely different strategy to game play with these Mahjong streak games you can play on the web, your typical tiles game will be changed over completely to a round of experience with the implantation of additional thrilling illustrations and extended components.

J'aime Mahjong has 80 different levels to tackle, made more engaging with inventive realistic plans. Silk road Mahjong's goal is to take out all comparative tiles on the board until it is cleared. Solitaire levels contain I Love Mahjong, like J'aime, with 80 levels to browse and to get high scores with. A more imaginative interpretation of the game is 10 Mahjong, where the matching of tiles don't just rely upon the similitude of stones, however the upsides of them expecting to amount to 10. Mahjong Disclosure is a 3D variant of the exemplary Chinese game ensured to improve the game play. On the off chance that you need a cuter, plot-based rendition, in any case, play Hubbo Mahjong HK, where the Hubbo group should battle against people in each Mahjong game to make due. Beside those referenced above, titles under this classification incorporate Mahjong Solitaire Challenge, Beijing Mahjong, Mahjong Nurseries and Wordsjong Free-form.

The unwinding and rationale prompting round of Mahjong just got considerably more energizing with its glimmer game partners! Play these games in a more daring methodology with additional vivified impacts and better system approaches in the solace of your screen.

CHAPTER FOUR

FEIGNING IN MAHJONG SHOULD BE POSSIBLE WITH YOUR TILES

Feigning is something that should be possible regardless of where you play mahjong. It is even conceivable online to Feign in mahjong. You can deal with feigning through your technique. This piece of feigning includes working with your tiles. While feigning in mahjong you ought to consider any good tiles that you have. You ought to then contemplate the same tiles that you have. It will help for you to not play your useful tiles early. This is a decent piece of feigning since individuals will believe that you have no good thing in your line. Driving individuals to believe that you have nothing is in every case great while feigning. One more part of feigning in mahjong includes disposing of any tiles that are good for you. This piece of feigning ought to work assuming you have tiles that are comparable to others in your column. You ought to utilize this system for feigning to make individuals believe that you are making some extreme memories tracking down great tiles. Nonetheless, you ought to work rapidly on the off chance that you dispose of tiles while feigning. This might be for the most part really great for feigning yet it can likewise be hurtful if you watch for how others could play your tiles. They could benefit off of what you had. Make certain to think about this while feigning in mahjong. The last part includes expanding your time in a move. Some of the time you may be sure about a move. You ought to disguise this feeling while feigning in mahjong by involving a greater amount of your time for a specific move. Feigning, in many games, can include you postponing your reaction to that conviction. This ought to work for feigning for of making individuals believe that you are unsure of what to do. Like most games, this can be an extraordinary methodology for feigning in mahjong.

FIGURING OUT MAHJONG ASSOCIATE

Mahjong interface is a variety of the famous mahjong solitaire. The two games include similar arrangement of tiles and offer a similar goal: clear the whole playing space by matching sets of indistinguishable tiles.

Mahjong interface is typically planned, which puts extra tension upon the player to think and act rapidly. The primary thing that recognizes mahjong associate from other mahjong game is the "interface" part. This implies that indistinguishable tiles must be eliminated from the board on the off chance that they can be "associated" by three or less straight lines.

This may a little confound from the start. Taking a gander at the game format, one could without much of a stretch perceive how you could define a straight boundary from any one tile to some other. Anyway, how does this standard truly work? It takes a tad of perception to comprehend these undetectable lines that associate the tiles in mahjong interface. The stunt is that you need to imagine defining a boundary from one tile to the next without cutting across some other tile. Most mahjong interface games will show you the lines that associate the tiles, yet solely after you have taken action. This can assist you with envisioning how the tiles associate. Assuming you are attempting to comprehend which tiles can be coordinated with which, simply pick arbitrary matching matches until you find coordinates that can be eliminated. Watch out for the lines that show up, generally momentarily, to perceive how the way is framed starting with one tile then onto the next. Three-line associations are generally normal, however one-and two-line ways can likewise be found.

One of the most supportive ways of figuring out mahjong interface is to envision that you are building a street. View at the unfilled space around the tiles as "open land." The actual tiles address deterrents perhaps structures or mountains. You can't clear your street through or over these obstructions you need to circumvent them. When you find a couple of coordinating, unblocked tiles, you really want to take a gander at the unfilled space around them to check whether you can define three or less straight boundaries to interface them.

An effective method for understanding this is to check two nearby indistinguishable tiles out. You can't simply define a boundary starting with one tile then onto the next. You want to go "out" into the "open land." In this way, you would define one boundary from the primary tile pointing straight the other way of the tile, then one more at a right point to the first, pointing toward the subsequent tile. Then, at that point, you would define a third boundary, opposite to the second and lined up with the first, driving back to the subsequent tile assuming you were to really define these boundaries on screen, it would seem to be a U-turn. It might take a couple of moves before the fledgling gets a decent handle of how to interface mahjong tiles, yet when you get its hang, mahjong associate is a superbly difficult and fun game.

THE END

Made in the USA
Las Vegas, NV
27 November 2023

81652762R00020